# Summary & Study Guide

# The Telomere Miracle

# Also by Lee Tang

Dual Momentum Trend Trading
Canada's Public Pension System Made Simple
**Summary & Study Guide Series:**

Brain Maker
The Gene
The Emperor of All Maladies
NeuroTribes
Brain Storms
The End of Diabetes
The End of Heart Disease
ADHD Nation
The Obesity Code
How Not to Die
Mind over Meds
A Crack in Creation
The Gene Machine
The Body Builders
Into the Gary Zone
Fat for Fuel
The Alzheimer's Solution
Healing Arthritis
Rise of the Necrofauna
We Are Our Brains
The Teenage Brain
The Better Brain Solution
The Plant Paradox
The Fountain
Resurrection Science
Sapiens
Homo Deus

The Beautiful Cure
The Diabetes Code
Brain Food
Anticancer Living
The End of Epidemics
The Rise and Fall of the
    Dinosaurs
10% Human
The Mind-Gut Connection
Civilization Microbia
An Elegant Defense
Cancerland
Empty Planet
The Longevity Paradox
Eat to Beat Disease
The Tangled Tree
The Body
The Spectrum of Hope
Memory Rescue
The Longevity Code
Healing Anxiety and Depres-
    sion
Healing ADD/ADHD
The Telomere Miracle
The Finance Curse

For a complete list of books by Lee Tang and information about the author, visit LMTPRESS.WORDPRESS.COM.

# Scientific Secrets to Fight Disease, Feel Great and Turn Back the Clock on Aging.

The must-read summary of "The Telomere Miracle: Scientific Secrets to Fight Disease, Feel Great and Turn Back the Clock on Aging," by Ed Park, MD.

Telomeres are long, repetitive sequences of DNA at the tips of our chromosomes to protect them from harm during cellular division. Every time a cell divides, the telomere shortens. When the telomeres are exhausted, cellular division stops and the cell dies.

Telomere erosion is a central driver of illness and aging. As our telomeres shorten, our whole body deteriorates, leading to a range of aging-related diseases, such as heart disease, diabetes, Alzheimer's disease, and dementia.

This book explains the many facets of human aging and shows you how to intervene in the aging process through lifestyle changes that boost the activity of the enzyme telomerase that lengthens your telomeres.

Apply what you learned from this book to win the war on aging, prevent chronic diseases, and live a longer, happier, healthier, and more productive life.

This guide includes:
- ❏ *Book Summary*—helps you understand the key concepts.
- ❏ *Online Videos*—cover the concepts in more depth.

Value-added from this guide:
- ❏ Save time
- ❏ Understand key concepts
- ❏ Expand your knowledge

## *Important Note About This Guide*

This guide is a summary and not a critique/review of the book. The summary may not be organized chapter-wise but summarizes the book's main ideas, viewpoints, and arguments. It is NOT meant to be a replacement, but a supplement to help you understand the book's key ideas and recommendations.

# Summary & Study Guide

# The Telomere Miracle

## Scientific Secrets to Fight Disease, Feel Great, and Turn Back the Clock on Aging

Lee Tang

LMT Press
LMTPRESS.WORDPRES.COM

**Title:** Summary & Study Guide - The Telomere Miracle
**Subtitle:** Scientific Secrets to Fight Disease, Feel Great, and Turn
Back the Clock on Aging
**Author:** Lee Tang
**Publisher:** LMT Press (lmtpress.wordpress.com)

First Edition: April 2020

Issued in print and electronic formats.
ISBN 9781988970363 (ebook)
ISBN 9781650429694 (paperback)
ISBN 9781078757362 (paperback)

*To my wife, Lillian, who is the source of energy and love for everything I do, and to Andrew and Amanda: watching you grow up has been a privilege.*

# Contents

# Part 1

## Aging Is Optional

# Chapter 1
# The Quest to End Aging

We all want to be healthy and stop aging. But do you know how and why we age? Once we have a better understanding of how and why we age, we will be better able to figure out how we can slow down the aging process.

The keys to understanding how and why we age are found in the growing body of telomere research. Dr. Ed Park has unified all these studies to come up with his *Telomere and Stem Cell Theory of Aging*, which will be explained in the next chapter. Here are the key points of the theory:

- ❏ Telomeres are long sequences of DNA at the tips of our cells' chromosomes to protect them from harm during cellular division.
- ❏ Every time a cell divides, the telomere shortens.
- ❏ Stem cells can restore telomere length with an enzyme called telomerase.
- ❏ The telomere length of a daughter cell can only be as long as the stem cell it came from.
- ❏ When telomeres become critically short, the cell malfunctions and/or dies from the resulting chromosome mutation. As a result, our whole body deteriorates, leading to a range of aging-related diseases, such as heart disease, diabetes, Alzheimer's disease, and dementia.

❏ The shortening of telomeres in stem cells causes aging.

Shorter telomeres have been associated with an increased incidence of aging-related diseases and decreased lifespan. Studies have shown that elderly people with shorter telomere lengths have a 20 percent increased risk of mortality. They are also three times more likely to die from heart disease and eight times more likely to die from infectious diseases.

Healthy adults inherit two copies of all genes (one from Mom and one from Dad). The result of inheriting one defective telomerase gene from one parent is a clinical condition called progeria, a rare genetic condition that causes a child's body to age fast. Most kids with progeria do not live past the age of 13.

Because all cells are derived from stem cells, if you have old and damaged stem cells, you will have old and damaged cells. Thanks to telomerase, we could preserve the telomeres in our stem cells to resist the aging process and reduce the risk of disease.

Studies have shown that specific lifestyle factors can increase or decrease the rate of telomere shortening. Better choice of diet and activities has great potential to reduce the rate of telomere shortening, delaying the onset of aging-related diseases and increasing lifespan. There are hundreds of scientific studies linking telomere health with six critical lifestyle factors: breathing, mindset, sleep, exercise, diet, and supplements. We call these factors the **TeloMirror Tools** (TMTs).

Think of the six TMTs as six cylinders in an engine. We should strive to optimize each of the TMTs to achieve maximal health.

Part 1 of this book will provide you with a crash course in cell biology and a unified theory of aging and disease. Part 2 will focus on the six TeloMirrow Tools. Part 3 will put the TMTs to use in your individualized plan.

# Online Videos

1. What is telomerase and what role does it play in aging? (https://youtu.be/iKI4ktJ0eTc)

2. What Are Telomeres and Why They Are Important in Anti-Aging (https://youtu.be/uqaR1q2trG8)

3. Telomerase Function (https://youtu.be/i6nE6gUp2cw)

# Chapter 2
# Biology 101—Genetics and Cell Biology

Each cell in the human body contains about six feet of DNA molecules spooled into tight packages called **chromosomes**. There are 23 pairs of chromosomes in its nucleus—one from each parent. **Telomeres** are long sequences of DNA at the tips of our chromosomes to protect them from harm during cellular divisions.

Segments of DNA in specific patterns are called **genes**. A gene is a basic physical unit of heredity. Only 3 percent of our DNA makes up our genes. The remaining 97 percent controls gene expression. Some genes store information for making proteins, but many do not code for proteins. The human genome is the complete collection of genes to code for all the proteins needed by the body to stay alive.

## DNA Replication: The Engine of Aging

A DNA molecule comprises two complementary "yin-yang" strands twisted around each other like a double helix. Each strand has a sugar/phosphate backbone. Attached to each sugar is one of four bases: adenine (A), thymine (T), guanine (G), or cytosine (C).

DNA's double helix structure makes it possible for the molecule to replicate. During replication, the double helix splits into two single helices—a leading strand and a lagging strand. Each of these single helices then turns into a double helix by assembling their complementary strands.

The leading strand can assemble its matching complementary strand with regular DNA. But the lagging strand must use a temporary RNA primer. Because the cell cannot attach the RNA primer to the very tip of the lagging strand, we lose a bit of telomere length every time the cell divides. Most cells can only replicate and divide forty to sixty times before they cannot divide anymore. The **Hayflick limit** is the number of times a normal human cell population will divide before cell division stops. It varies depending on the cell type and doesn't apply to stem cells and cancer cells because they can rebuild their telomeres using an enzyme called **telomerase**.

All plants and animals with linear chromosomes need telomeres. Bacteria don't need telomeres because they have circular chromosomes and hence have no ends to protect. That's why they can replicate billions of times without dying.

## How Genes Make Proteins

Proteins are the building blocks of our cells and are essential for every function taking place within the body. This includes maintaining healthy tissues, assembling hormones, and powering chemical reactions. They are made of long chains of amino acids based on instructions in our genes. The order of the base pairs in each gene specifies the sequence of amino acids that make up the protein.

Cells need to assemble and update their proteins constantly for optimal structure and function. Cell function, or dysfunction, depends on having the correct protein made.

# Epigenetics: Why Cells are Different Despite Having the Same DNA

Every cell in your body contains the same DNA, so all your cells could produce 20,000 or more proteins encoded in your DNA. But they don't. Our body has many cell types and each cell type deploys its genome differently. This process of gene expression is regulated by cues from both within and outside the cells. The interplay between these cues and the genome affects all processes that occur during embryonic development and adult life. Epigenetic modifications to the DNA don't alter the DNA sequences but dictate which proteins will be expressed.

# Stem Cells—The Secret of Immortality

Most of our body's cells are **differentiated cells**, meaning they perform specific functions, such as liver cells and skin cells.

**Stem cells** provide new cells for the body as it grows and replace differentiated cells that are damaged or lost. The differentiated daughter cells created by stem cells live regular cell lives. They divide to make regular cells and are subject to the Hayflick limit.

There is a master stem cell type, called **mesenchymal stem cells** (MSCs), that can travel to all organs to replace worn-out or dead stem cells. These MSCs are less specialized and will undergo on-the-job training to take on the role of an adult stem cell.

Our immortal stem cells cannot keep us young forever because of these issues:

❏ **Telomerase can't keep up with its task.** Perhaps it is your stress, lack of exercise, poor sleep, or chronic inflammation that is hindering your stem cells from repairing.

❏ **DNA errors and damage occur in the actual genes between the telomere caps.** Here genetic information gets damaged by transcription errors, viruses, radiation, and toxins, which cause irregularities in cell functioning because of gene mutation or functional deletion. If the damaged stem cells reproduce, their dysfunction can manifest as diseases because all the cells from that stem cell have the same genetic problems.

❏ **The reserve of backup MSCs can become damaged and depleted.**

## Telomerase Reverses Aging

You can't take telomerase orally because it is a large protein which would be digested by the acid in your digestive system. You can't inject telomerase because it's too big to diffuse into cells for use. The only effective way to activate telomerase is to do healthy things that enhance its functioning inside your body.

## Online Videos

1. DNA replication (https://youtu.be/TNKWgcFPHqw)

2. Telomerase Function (https://youtu.be/i6nE6gUp2cw)

3. DNA, Hot Pockets, & The Longest Word Ever (https://youtu.be/itsb2SqR-R0)

4. What is Gene Expression? (https://youtu.be/7-D63BWemIM)

5. Stem Cells (https://youtu.be/i2pyDBMglfM)

6. Telomeres and cell senescence (https://youtu.be/R5YiO6rKr-w)

7. What is telomerase and what role does it play in aging? (https://youtu.be/iKI4ktJ0eTc)

8. Why We Age - And How We Can Stop It (https://youtu.be/jqCo-McgHLw)

# Chapter 3
# Aging—One Cause, One Cure

Ask people to describe aging and they might tell you about the normal signs of aging: wrinkles, gray hair, a slightly stooped posture, perhaps some "senior moments" of forgetfulness. Or, they might give you a list of symptoms, conditions, or diseases: decrease in overall energy, reduced reflexes, hearing losses, cataracts, osteoporosis, and memory loss.

Some anti-aging gurus proposed that aging was caused by free radicals and oxidative damage and that taking antioxidants is the cure. This was proven wrong when a McGill University study found that antioxidant-depleted worms lived 30 percent longer than those with active antioxidants. Other studies showed that supplementing with antioxidants didn't postpone aging, and might harm your health.

People experience similar problems as they get older because they are all made up of cells containing the same genetic material and operating by the same biological rules. The following studies suggest that all these signs, symptoms, and diseases of aging result from DNA damage caused by the telomere shortening that occurs in stem cells.

❏ A study published in the journal *Psychoneuroendocrinology* found low telomerase activity was associated with elevated **stress** hormones, **smoking**, **high blood pressure**, **high blood sugar**, and excessive **belly**

**fat**. Based on all the health issues noted, the researchers concluded that low telomerase is an early marker of **heart-disease risk**.

❏ Researchers from the University of Medicine and Dentistry and St. Thomas Hospital in London found that *lean* women had longer telomeres, while *overweight* women had much shorter ones. They concluded that maintaining a healthy weight preserves the health of your telomeres.

❏ A study published in *Arthritis Research and Therapy* found that osteoarthritic patients had shorter telomeres when compared with adults without arthritis, and the telomere length appeared progressively shorter in the cells that were closer to the arthritic area.

❏ A study published in *Osteoporosis International* found that women who were at risk for **osteoporosis** and had poorer **bone density** had shorter telomeres than women who were at lower risk for the condition. The study concluded that telomere length is a likely marker of bone aging.

❏ When Harvard researchers genetically engineered mice that lack the ability to produce telomerase, they saw accelerated symptoms of aging, including organ failure, tissue injury, gray hair, and wrinkled skin. When they reactivated the enzyme in these mice, they saw the aging reversing effects of telomerase: gray hair became dark, wrinkled skin smoothed and plumped, energy returned, and organs regained function.

❏ In a longevity study published in the *Proceedings of the National Academy of Sciences*, researchers found that centenarians had higher telomerase activity compared to those who died at younger ages.

# Key Points to Remember

- ❏ **Tools in this book are called TeloMirror Tools** because science has shown that your lifestyle choices benefit the health of your telomeres.

- ❏ **Because of the mechanics of DNA replication**, telomeres always shorten when cells divide.

- ❏ **Ordinary non-stem cells must die**. We call this the Hayflick limit, and it serves to protect us from rogue cells that have become mutated or defective.

- ❏ **Stem cells can regrow shortened telomeres** with telomerase. They can live forever. When damaged stem cells don't die off, we get dysfunctional cells and are prone to cancer and disease.

- ❏ **Telomeres are dynamic**. They can lengthen or shorten in stem cells depending on telomerase activation and environmental effects (your lifestyle).

- ❏ **Ordinary cells cannot be younger or healthier** than their most recent stem cell parents.

- ❏ **The health of your stem cells** determines the health of your cells and organs.

- ❏ **The shortening of telomeres in stem cells** causes aging, but it can be mitigated if telomeres in stem cells have adequate telomerase activation.

In the next six chapters, we will examine the TeloMirror Tools that play an essential role in slowing down the shortening of your telomeres.

# Online Videos

1. The Key to Chromosome Immortality
   (https://youtu.be/f-JLnfnGPyA)
2. The science of cells that never get old
   (https://youtu.be/2wseM6wWd74)

# Part 2

## TeloMirrors—The Tools That Turn Back Time

# Chapter 4
## Your Breath

You can survive 3 weeks without food, 3 days without water, but only 3 minutes without air. That makes breathing the top TMT. However, most of us don't worry about how we breathe until we have an illness that limits our ability to breathe.

The two main reasons for breathing are to take in oxygen ($O_2$) and to expel carbon dioxide ($CO_2$). When you inhale air into your lungs, your lungs pass oxygen into your bloodstream. Your cells use oxygen from your blood to convert glucose in your cells into energy that powers the cell's chemical machinery. This cellular respiration produces $CO_2$. When you exhale, you rid your blood of the accumulated $CO_2$.

$CO_2$ builds up as carbonic acid in your body and lowers the pH levels in your blood, making it more acidic. When your blood's pH value falls outside of 7.35 to 7.45, the brainstem will adjust your breathing to balance the pH value of the blood. If you hold your breath, you will receive signals from the brain when your $CO_2$ levels are too high. These signals include strong, painful, and involuntary contractions or spasms of the diaphragm and the muscles between your ribs. That's why it's difficult to hold your breath for long.

When you inhale much deeper and take much faster breaths than normal, you blow out too much $CO_2$. This is called **hyperventilating**, and it can disrupt the balance of $O_2$ and $CO_2$ in your body, resulting in dizziness, tingling, muscle spasms, and other distressing symptoms.

Swimmers who are training to hold their breath for longer times intentionally breathe rapidly to blow off $CO_2$ and raise their blood pH. This can fool their brain into thinking it need not take another breath. If this happens, their body can quickly use up most of its available oxygen, causing the swimmer to lose consciousness. If this occurs underwater, the swimmer is at a serious risk of drowning.

## The Mechanics and Muscles of Breathing

There are three ways to inhale, in order of decreasing efficiency:

- ❑ **Diaphragmatic Breathing**. Drop your diaphragm to create a vacuum to suck in the air.
- ❑ **Chest Breathing**. Use the muscles between the ribs to expand the rib cage to create a vacuum to suck in air.
- ❑ **Neck Breathing**. Use the accessory muscles in your neck and shoulders to lift the rib cage to suck in air.

When we are sleeping or exercising, we breathe efficiently using our diaphragm. When we are self-consciously inhaling, we use our chest and rib breathing. When we are anxious, we use our accessory muscles, resulting in shoulder and neck pain.

Breathing out is often the result of passive recoil in your elastic rib cage after being stretched outward. But the diaphragm and abdominal muscles between the ribs can also help to expel more air.

## What Does Telomere Science Tell Us About Breathing?

Scientists who study telomeres and lung function have found a relationship between better breathing and longer telomeres.

They have also found a link between diseases of the respiratory system, shorter telomeres, and lower telomerase activity.

- ❏ Johns Hopkins University researchers found that people with a condition known as idiopathic pulmonary fibrosis (IPF) have telomerase mutated genes and shorter telomeres. IPF causes scar tissue to grow inside your lungs and makes it hard to breathe.
- ❏ Researchers have shown that they can reverse the effects of IPF when they introduced a telomerase activator to mice with the condition.
- ❏ Johns Hopkins University researchers found telomerase and telomere gene mutations in smokers with a lung condition that causes shortness of breath.
- ❏ Danish researchers found that shorter telomere lengths are 28 times more common in those with chronic obstructive pulmonary disease (COPD) than in those who don't have this lung disease.
- ❏ Studies have shown that both COPD and asthma were correlated with shorter telomere length.

## Is There a Wrong Way to Breathe?

When asked to take a deep breath, you'd likely expand your chest and suck up your diaphragm, causing your belly to suck in. The correct way is to drop your diaphragm to create a vacuum to suck in air, causing your belly to protrude rather than retract.

Breathing through your mouth dries it out, which causes poor oral hygiene, bad breath, and cavities. If you are breathing through your mouth, perhaps because of blocked nasal passages, you are not getting three crucial benefits of nose breathing: warming, humidifying, and filtering of particles.

When you are anxious, you don't take full, loud belly breaths. You just use your neck muscles to take shallow sips of air. This puts constant tension on your neck and ends up causing chronic headaches, numb and tingling hands, neck pain, or upper back pain.

When you are depressed, your posture tends to collapse. Poor posture can cause neck breathing. If your spine is not aligned, the abdomen and chest are constricted and unable to expand properly, causing you to breathe with your neck muscles.

The simplest way to improve breathing is by maintaining good posture. This means maintaining an erect posture and sitting up straight while seated. Sleep on your back is preferred, as lying on your side creates some lateral compression of the rib cage. Many people have obstructive sleep apnea, so if that is a problem, correct it with a continuous positive airway pressure machine (CPAP).

# Breathing Exercises—Teaching Yourself How to Breathe

### 1. "Square" Breathing to Improve Focus

Practice this exercise after you wake up in the morning, or after a nap.

- ❏ Sit or lie down.
- ❏ Relax and place one hand on your chest and the other on your belly.
- ❏ Inhale slowly through your nose and feel the hand on your belly rise and move outward.
- ❏ Pause for 5 or 6 counts at the top of your inhale.
- ❏ Exhale slowly for 5 or 6 counts. Feel your belly move inwards as you press gently with your hand on your belly.
- ❏ Pause for 5 or 6 counts at the bottom of your exhale to complete the square, then start again.

## 2. "4-7-8" Hold-Breath Technique to Relax

This technique is useful for calming general stress or anxiety.

- ❏ Exhale completely through your mouth.
- ❏ Close your mouth and inhale slowly through your nose for 4 seconds.
- ❏ At the top of you inhale, hold your breath and count slowly to 7.
- ❏ Exhale slowly through your mouth, counting to 8.

Repeat three more times for a total of four breaths.

## 3. Paper-Bag Breathing to Counteract Hyperventilation

This is useful when experiencing hyperventilation and dizziness accompanying moderate-to-severe anxiety or panic attacks.

- ❏ Hold a small paper bag over your mouth and nose.
- ❏ Inhale slowly.
- ❏ Exhale slowly.

Repeat for 6 to 12 breaths, until your anxiety recedes.

## 4. Heart Breathing for Bliss

Sit down and close your eyes. Place your left hand on your belly and the right hand on your heart. With each inhalation, imagine that your breath is flowing in and out of your heart. Summon a memory of a peaceful place and smile.

- ❏ Inhale for 5 seconds, thinking, "Love is..."
- ❏ Exhale for 5 seconds, thinking,"...everywhere."

Repeat for 15 to 20 seconds. You can make up any mantra you like.

### 5. Breath of Fire to Increase Energy

- ❏ Sit down, either cross-legged or in a chair with feet grounded.
- ❏ Until you become proficient, you can place one or both of your hands on your abdomen.
- ❏ Exhale only through your nose with brief bursts of diaphragmatic elevations. The bursts should be 2 per second for 25 breaths.
- ❏ Inhalation is passive
- ❏ Exhale it all out.
- ❏ Repeat, while holding each of the following locks:
  - ■ Make a tight contraction of your pelvic floor (like you want to hold it in a full bladder).
  - ■ Pull your navel in and up.
  - ■ Breathe into your chest and tuck your chin into your chest.

## Other Ways to Breath Young

### Move for Better Breathing

How to breathe during cardio vs. strength training:

- ❏ **During strength training**: It is dangerous to hold your breath while exerting effort on a weight. It is better to inhale as you stretch or load the muscles and to exhale as you contract or flex your muscles.
- ❏ **While doing cardio**: Begin breathing through your nose during your warm-up, and then when your intensity ramps up, you'll breathe through your nose and mouth. Let it happen—this gets more oxygen to your lungs and the rest of your body to meet the demands of your body.

### Correct Posture for Better Breathing

Sitting hunched at a desk for long periods of time can cause neck breathing. If your job requires hours at a desk, set a timer to remind you to sit up with your shoulders rolled back and down, and to keep both feet on the floor. You can also consider standing desks, kneeling chairs, or chairs with adjustable seat-backs. Just make sure you aren't slouched over and making breathing more difficult by collapsing our rib cage.

### Mindful Breathing

See chapter 5.

### Clean Air Acts

Ensure a healthy breathing environment. During times of the year when plants release pollen and other allergens into the air, keep windows closed, or use air filters. Older houses and leaky plumbing are risk factors for a home infection with fungus or mold that could harm you.

## Online Videos

1. What is Chronic Obstructive Pulmonary Disease (COPD)? (https://youtu.be/gf6n8ybwmvE)
2. CNIO researchers cure lung fibrosis in mice with a gene therapy that lengthens telomeres (https://youtu.be/caFzqORoBv0)
3. Deep Breathing Exercises for Beginners (https://youtu.be/acUZdGd_3Dg)
4. 3 Deep Breathing Exercises to Reduce Stress & Anxiety (https://youtu.be/sJ04nsiz_M0)
5. Importance of BREATHING During Workout (https://youtu.be/rDVydqQw_Sg)
6. 3 Breathing Techniques To Use When Lifting Weight (https://youtu.be/IYCZKyQRyUE)

# Chapter 5
# Your Mind

To interact with others, it is important to understand their mental states and to think about how those mental states might influence their actions. Theory of mind is the ability to understand the desires, intentions, and beliefs of others, and is a skill that a typical young child develops between 3 and 5 years of age. People with autism and narcissistic personality disorder have difficulty understanding other peoples' mental states because they are underdeveloped in their theory of mind.

Humans and other social animals have "mirror neurons" that "mirrors" the behavior of others, as though the observer were itself acting. Mirror neurons enable us to reflect body language, facial expressions, and emotions. They allow us to learn through imitation and to understand the intentions behind actions.

When the brain stores a memory of an event or action, it also stores an associated emotion with it. This is what we call "emotional tagging." We can't control what happens to us, but we can choose what stories, emotions, and importance we assign to our memories. The key to mastering the mind is to master the emotional tagging of all that you perceive. Whether facing a true threat, a joke, or a memory, we must always exercise control over our emotions. Accept the things you can't change, and change the things you can.

# What Does Telomere Science Say About the Mind and Stress?

Stress stimulates the body to release the stress hormone cortisol that brings about a flight-or-fight response. If we allow stress to dominate our lives, the long-term effects of high cortisol levels include increased risk for diabetes, obesity, poor immune function, osteoporosis, infertility, stomach ulcers, and more. These studies show that chronic stress and high levels of cortisol shorten your telomeres.

❏ A 2008 study published in the journal *Brain, Behaviour, and Immunity* found that cortisol inhibits telomerase activity in our T cells, weakening our immune system. Weaker immunity encourages chronic infections like cytomegalovirus (CMV) that age us and make it harder to eliminate damaged and cancerous cells.

❏ A study published in the Proceedings of the National Academy of Sciences showed that high stress is associated with shorter telomeres.

❏ Researchers at the University of California-San Francisco (UCSF) found that when men followed a comprehensive plan including stress reduction techniques that incorporated breathing and mindfulness training, they decreased the age of their cells (as shown by telomere-lengthening) by more than a decade. These strategies also boost serotonin and melatonin to increase relaxation and reduce the stress hormone cortisol.

❏ Having close social ties may lengthen telomeres and extend lives.

❏ When researchers at UCSF attempted to teach obese women mindful eating, body awareness, meditation, and yoga, they found that even women in the control

group who didn't receive the treatment benefited because of the placebo effect.

❏ Chronic stress produces adrenal exhaustion, which
leads to low cortisol levels. The effect can be anxiety
and depression, which leads to low telomerase activity. Low telomere activity can lead to telomere shortening, mutation, cell apoptosis, and inflammation and
oxidation that people misconstrue as the cause instead
of the effect.

# How to Use Your Mind to Stay Young

There are many ways to elevate telomerase activity by harnessing
a positive and healing mindset.

## The Pursuit of Happiness

Psychologist Mihaly Csikszentmihalyi discovered that people find
genuine satisfaction during a state of consciousness called **Flow**.
In this state, they are absorbed in an activity that involves their
creative abilities. During this state, they feel "strong, alert, in ef-
fortless control, unselfconscious, and at the peak of their abilities."

Life would include three separate aspects of happiness: plea-
sures, immersion (or flow), and meaning. Pleasure and immersion cannot fulfill us when there is little meaning. We are not
happy with just immersion and meaning if we don't find the
work pleasurable. And pleasure and meaning wouldn't fulfill us
if we can't relax and go with the flow of the act of procreation.
**Pleasure + meaning + flow = fulfillment**. It's like a three-legged
stool: take away one leg and you lose stability.

## Take Control of Automatic Thoughts

When people receive negative thoughts about themselves, they
remember it in their subconscious mind. Unless they talk back to
these harmful thoughts, they believe them even though the

thoughts may be irrational. Automatic negative thoughts are automatic thoughts that can lie to you to make situations worse than they are. These thoughts can affect your feelings, moods, and behaviors, leading to anxiety and depression.

### Remodel and Replace Harmful Beliefs

Our early childhood experiences shape our minds and play a large role in how we interact with the world. If a child had an abusive and alcoholic parent, she may become a toxic parent to her child.

In contrast, a child who is told he or she is special and always receives unearned praise and exceptional treatment may become narcissistic and poorly integrated into society. Such children have a false belief that they are special, and when the world doesn't reward them with favors, they fail.

Letting go of the unproductive core beliefs you developed during childhood can be the key to moving forward and reaching your greatest potential.

# How to Improve Your Mindfulness

If we nurture negative thinking patterns, we will manifest counterproductive beliefs and behaviors and cause a downward spiral, allowing our telomeres to shorten. Negative thoughts lead to impaired breathing, insomnia, depression, disinterest in exercise, emotional overeating, and so on. In contrast, upward spiral results when we reframe these beliefs by practicing positive thinking. Here are some ways to improve your mindfulness:

### TMT Mind-Hack #1: The Quick Fix Is Just to Breathe

If you haven't mastered the ability to be in the present moment, then focusing on breathing always brings you back. Sit down somewhere quiet and just breathe—eyes open, eyes closed, with or without holding your breath. All is good as long as you are consciously breathing into your abdomen.

## TMT Mind-Hack #2: Laughter Is an Orgasm of the Soul

Laughter works two TMTs at once: breathing and consciousness. I recommend keeping a brief comedy skit that always makes you laugh on your smartphone or computer.

## TMT Mind Hack #3: Use Meditation to Deal with Negative Thoughts

You can use meditation to distance yourself from destructive negative thoughts and even create "antidote mantras" to negate them. There are many ways to meditate. Experiment to find what works best for you. To get started, try this simple meditation.

- ❏ Sit or lie down. Set a timer for five minutes.
- ❏ Close your eyes and breathe naturally.
- ❏ Focus your attention on the breath and on how the body moves with each inhalation and exhalation.
- ❏ When you notice that your mind has drifted from your breath, smile to yourself, and bring your attention back to your breath.

## TMT Mind-Hack #4: Use C.A.R.E. to Refurbish Those Old Beliefs

- ❏ **Clear the clutter in your life**. You might be surprised to know how infrequently others think about you.
- ❏ **Audit the voices.** Listen to the demons in your head and create an antidote mantra or positive self-talk. Look in the mirror, stand up straight, smile, and say, "I choose to be happy at this moment."
- ❏ **Reframe.** Reframing involves changing your perspective on a situation to give it a more positive or benefi-

cial meaning to you. You can use reframing to help remove limiting beliefs, to help appreciate positive moments that you might otherwise miss, or for any other negative thoughts you would like to change.

❏ **Enjoy.** Enjoying each moment will bring better focus, attract more luck and better people.

## Online Videos

1. Robert Seyfarth: Theory of Mind (https://youtu.be/XDtjLSa50uk)

2. The Mirror Neuron System: Understanding Others as Oneself (https://youtu.be/DY1HAJGpyVw)

3. Automatic Thoughts (https://youtu.be/m2zRA5zCA6M)

4. 3 Quick Steps to Stop Negative Thinking Now! (https://youtu.be/ksB0IXhM-Vc)

5. How To Think About Negative Thoughts (https://youtu.be/8ZnSLt4deXo)

6. 5-Minute Meditation You Can Do Anywhere (https://youtu.be/inpok4MKVLM)

# Chapter 6
# Your Sleep

Sleep is a necessary biological function. During sleep, the brain performs two important functions:

❏ Detoxification of amyloid and oxidative by-products;
❏ Consolidation of memory and thought. Convert short-term memories into long-term memories. Remove un-needed memories, organize thought processes, and build new connections.

Sleep deprivation and dysfunction impair learning and neural plasticity. Lack of sleep leads us to insomnia, legal and illegal drug use, mood disorders, and suicidal ideation.

In 1989, researchers at the University of Chicago showed that rats die when deprived of sleep for 32 days. Research shows that sleep deprivation in humans impairs learning and neural plasticity, and is associated with mental and mood problems, immune dysfunction, diabetes, cardiovascular disease, substance abuse, suicidal ideation, and shorter lifespans.

## Sleep Cycles

Each night we pass through an average of four to six 90-minute sleep cycles. Each cycle passes through four stages classified into two general classes: rapid eye movement (REM) and Non-REM. Once you reach the end of a 90-minute cycle, you wake up briefly, even if you are unaware of it, then head down to your next cycle.

The sleep cycle proceeds in this order and lasts 90 minutes:

**Stage 1 → Stage 2 → Stage 3 → REM Stage → Stage 1**

- ❏ **Stage 1 (Non-REM)** (about 10 minutes): Your eyes are closed, but it's easy to wake you up. There is a moderate loss of muscle tone and conscious awareness during this stage.

- ❏ **Stage 2 (Non-REM)** (about 40 minutes): You are in light sleep. Your heart rate slows, and your body temperature drops. Your body is getting ready for deep sleep.

- ❏ **Stage 3 (Non-REM)** (about 20 minutes): This is the deep sleep stage. Your body is paralyzed, and it's harder to rouse you during this stage. During this deep sleep stage, the body repairs tissues, builds bone and muscle, strengthens the immune system, and clears the amyloid and oxidative by-products accumulated during the day. It is during this phase that **parasomnias** like sleepwalking, bedwetting, and night terrors can occur,

- ❏ **REM Stage** (about 20 minutes): REM sleep is characterized by eye movement, increased respiration rate, and increased brain activity. REM sleep allows the brain to prioritize procedural memories into stories, sequences, or skills to be integrated into the larger neural network.

## Declarative versus Procedural Memory

Declarative memory allows us to consciously recollect events and facts, such as faces, numbers, and names. Procedural memory (or nondeclarative memory), in contrast, is accessed without consciousness rather than recollection.

During stages 2 and 3, your brain converts short-term declarative memories into long-term memories by creating new brain cells and prioritizes information according to their emotional importance.

REM sleep is where active learning happens. During REM sleep, the brain prioritizes procedural memories and assembles the information into stories, sequences, or skills. REM sleep makes sense of memories by constructing stories around them. If you filter your world with fear and scarcity, you'd have a nightmare. However, if your mind is flowing with gratitude, you will have a wonderful dream. By using techniques like the C.A.R.E. method (chapter 5), we can leverage our dream life so that the procedural REM dream function can make us better beliefs.

So during REM sleep, your mind works on your subconscious "issues" and manufactures meaning and narratives around the emotional turmoil of the waking life. If you can't complete this task, it will be difficult to adjust to life's changes because you'll remain stuck in old stories about the world. This leads to addictions, mood problems, and a poor quality of life.

### Neuroplasticity

Sleep doesn't just strengthen learning and memories. It also prunes the brain's synapses by removing unneeded memories, organizing thought processes, and building new connections. Without the **neuroplasticity** of non-REM sleep, you would struggle to make new memories and erase old ones. Your memory would be jumbled and inefficient and you'd lack focus and make mistakes. **Fatal familial insomnia** (FFI) is a rare genetic degenerative brain disorder characterized by insomnia that may be initially mild but progressively worsens, leading to significant physical and mental deterioration.

## Obstacles to Getting Good Sleep

### Anatomy

**Obstructive sleep apnea** (OSA) is the most common anatomical reason for disrupted sleep, affecting 50 percent of middle-aged men. The problem arises when you lose active muscle tone while unconscious—the airway closes, causing difficulty breathing, and waking you up many times an hour. Symptoms include daytime sleepiness, loud snoring, and restless sleep. Studies have shown that people with OSA have shorter telomeres, racing heartbeats, cardiac stress, and an increased risk of heart attacks.

You can treat sleep apnea by losing weight if you're obese, and by sleeping on your side. If these fixes don't work, you can use a CPAP (continuous positive airway pressure) machine. I don't recommend surgery for sleep apnea because of the low cure rate, scarring, pain, and changes in your voice.

## Anxiety

If your mind is burdened with anxiety, your moments of brief wakefulness between sleep cycles can make it hard to go back to sleep. The solution? Try combining Chapter 4's TMT Breathing Exercises with Chapter 5's TeloMirror Mind-Hacks. Breathe in with the thought, "I am," and breathe out with the thought, "enough." Next, use the C.A.R.E. approach to create antidotes for negative stories.

## Ambien (zolpidem)

You should avoid this class of sleeping aids because they are dangerous and addictive. An over-the-counter antihistamine like Benadryl or Unisom is okay. If you are changing time zones, taking melatonin is helpful.

## Alcohol

Research shows that consuming alcohol before bed can disrupt your sleep. Alcohol can cause sexual dysfunction, dehydration, and produce a temporary inhibition of glutamine. Hours after you've had a drink, glutamine rebounds, causing an increased level of arousal by suppressing the production of GABA, a relaxing neurotransmitter you need for sleep.

### *Alarm Clock*

If you stay up late partying on the weekends and use the alarm clock to wake you up, you are inviting circadian rhythm disruption. It is important to go to sleep early enough so you can get at least five cycles of sleep. If you are healthy, your body's natural circadian rhythm will wake you in between cycles. When you set your alarm, calculate for eight and a half hours, and set the tone for an extra 10 to 15 minutes past your planned time. Use a gentle tone, so your mind and body will have time to wake up, rather than being jolted back into consciousness by a loud buzzer.

## Telomere Science and Sleep

Common themes linking sleep dysfunction with telomere dysfunction include:

- ❏ Lack of sleep is associated with shorter telomeres.
- ❏ Both quality and quantity of sleep matter.
- ❏ Snoring shortens telomeres

## Putting Your Sleep TeloMirror Tool to Work

### *1. Sleep with Gratitude*

Every night, host a "top 10 things I'm grateful for" countdown in your mind before sleep. These seeds of thoughts, feelings, and beliefs you implant right before sleep will grow into whatever you sow while dreaming. Plant better thoughts before sleep and you will grow better beliefs.

## 2. Waking with Purpose.

Before opening your eyes, acknowledge that a new day has be-
gun, then take a few breaths and visualize how it will feel and
look like to do the wonderful things you have planned for your
day.

## 3. Check Your Basic Sleep Hygiene

- ❏ **Sights**. Go dark, get quiet. Bright light—from screens,
  lamps, street light outside your window, or the clock
  on your bedside table—is an impediment to sleep.
  Eliminate as many sources of bright light in your bed-
  room as possible. Try a sleep mask.

- ❏ **Sounds**. Listening to soothing music before you sleep
  can help reduce stress and anxiety, help you fall
  asleep, and even improve the quality of your sleep. If
  noise is a problem, use earplugs.

- ❏ **Smells**. There shouldn't be any old smells in your
  sleep environment. Many people find the scent of
  lavender essential oil relaxing.

- ❏ **Touch**. Sleep with breathable sheets and light com-
  forters. Get a decent mattress and a high-quality pillow. Keep the air cool, but your hands and feet warm.

- ❏ **Feel (or Sleep Positioning)**. If you sleep on your back,
  have pillows under your knees to take the pressure off
  your lower back. If you sleep on your side, have
  a pillow between your knees to keep pressure off
  your lower back.

- ❏ **Taste**. Because of mouth breathing and failure to swal-
  low saliva, the normal cleansing of the mouth
  doesn't occur while sleeping. This can lead to bacterial overgrowth and "morning breath." You can keep
  a bit of water to drink next to your bed to keep your
  mouth cleaner.

# Online Videos

1. What a Good Night's Sleep Does for the Brain (https://youtu.be/WpkfMuXJnWI)

2. Why Sleep is critical for the Body and Brain | Science of Sleep (https://youtu.be/oTlJnyF3REs)

3. Why Sleep Matters? (https://youtu.be/LmwgGkJ64CM)

4. Sleep, Memory, and Dreams (https://youtu.be/XUA3fL4mzhg)

5. The Power of Dreams and Memories (https://youtu.be/a_sNos4Po58)

6. Understanding Obstructive Sleep Apnea (https://youtu.be/wmC8jMS16NI)

7. Getting Good Sleep (https://youtu.be/s_1uiMB7Obk)

# Chapter 7
# Your Exercise

S tudies have shown that exercise produces extraordinary benefits. A little stress from exercise improves the strength and resilience of your bones, cartilage, ligaments, joints, and muscles. Damage and inflammation in sore muscles from strength training prompt niche muscle stem cells to produce more muscle cells, as long as you don't push too hard. Exercise also stimulates muscle proliferation in the heart and arteries. Research suggests a direct link between low oxygen levels triggered by aerobic exercise and increased telomerase activity.

Optimal functioning for exercise varies from person to person. It boils down to finding out what sort of exercise works for you. That means identifying what is enjoyable, safe, but also challenging. Whatever your physical performance needs or aspirations may be, your body will adapt as long as you have decent stem cells to replace damaged ones.

There are three major components to consider when choosing exercises:

❏ Include some cardiovascular challenges.
❏ Stress your muscles, allowing for some days of recovery.
❏ Encourage flexibility without inducing injury.

Other considerations include exercising in ways that allow you to spend time with people and pets you love, to meet new people and socialize, to release stress and focus the mind, and to get some sunlight to make vitamin D.

## Cardiovascular Training or "Cardio"

This category means exercise for the heart and lungs. Typical cardio activities include brisk walking, running, biking, and swimming. Cardio gets your heart racing and makes you sweat. Swimming is the best cardio as you get older because of the low levels of stress on joints.

## Pumping Iron

Resistance training includes simple calisthenics (push-ups, sit-ups, and jumping jacks), lifting weights, kettlebells, dumbbells, free weights, machine resistance, and interval training (alternating bursts of activities with rest periods).

Most experts recommend weight training only three times a week unless you are rotating the body areas. The breakdown of muscles requires at least two days of recovery to be of maximum benefit. It is during rest times that the stem cells are making your muscles and tissues bigger and stronger. Patients can decrease this recovery time and increase healing efficiency when they take telomerase activators or adaptogens.

## Yoga

Yoga is a meditation based on conscious breathing while moving through static poses. You can modify it to any level of fitness, strength, and flexibility. Studies have shown that yoga is superior to many other forms of back pain treatment.

# Common Problems with Exercise.

❑ **Sudden death.** In this scenario, a middle-aged, sedentary man drops dead from a massive heart attack when he exercises. Give your body a chance to adjust to a higher level of challenge or risk injury or worse. Always get evaluated for palpitations, persistent shortness of breath, excessive fatigue, tingling and numbness, nausea, and persistent pain.

❑ **Injury.** Challenge yourself but always pay attention to your body. Know the difference between muscle fatigue and pain. Pain is inflammation from injury and is a warning to stop doing what you are doing. If you ignore and push through pain, you will be prone to injuries.

❑ **Inadequate recovery time.** Strength training involves muscle destruction. Without recovery, more exercise is just more destruction. We need time to heal to benefit from exercise, and sleep is the prime time for growth hormones and cell replication to take place.

❑ **Boredom and lack of discipline.** We often overcomplicate, ritualize, procrastinate, and create imaginary barriers to fitness. If everyone did a few dozen push-ups and sit-ups with good technique and some stretching, that might take about five minutes a day.

# Telomere Science and Exercise

❑ A large 2015 cohort study showed that many exercises were associated with longer telomeres.

❑ A study showed that the effects of exercise become more powerful and critical after age 42.

❑ A 2015 study found that the ability to walk long distances and have powerful leg strength were correlated with increased telomere length.

- ❏ A 2010 study suggested that the oxygen-carrying capacity of the subject was the only variable correlated with telomere length.

- ❏ A 2003 study found that athletes with **Fatigued Athlete Myopathic Syndrome (FAMS)** have shorter telomeres, suggesting that when you overdo exercise, the muscle stem cells were so busy copying that they didn't have time to regrow the length.

- ❏ Studies have concluded that there is a "U-shaped" curve between exercise and benefits. Too little exercise is bad, but too much, as with FAMS, is also bad.

- ❏ A 2008 study showed moderation was best. Telomere length was best in those who didn't overdo it or neglect their exercise.

## Get the Most Out of Your TeloMirror Exercise Tool

Research shows that exercise is most critical after age 42. You should exercise in moderation that includes strength training and an aerobic challenge. A good goal would be to make sure you are strengthening your legs and using your breathing capacity. Give yourself adequate recovery time and don't exercise a joint or muscle that is still in pain. Here are some ways to incorporate more exercise into your telomere preserving routine.

- ❏ **Pick a social activity—or not**. Some people prefer to exercise alone. Other folks crave variety and social interaction.

- ❏ **Make it a mindful routine**. Some mindful movements are yoga, tai chi, and qi gong. If you are doing cardio exercises, varying the intensity with interspersed rest periods (interval training) adds focus and improves the efficiency of what you're doing.

- ❏ **Create a habit**. You can set up a cue, routine, and reward to remind you to exercise.

# Online Videos

1. Many Benefits of Exercise
   (https://youtu.be/IASpJA5NPFg)

2. What happens inside your body when you exercise?
   (https://youtu.be/wWGulLAa000)

3. The brain-changing benefits of exercise
   (https://youtu.be/BHY0FxzoKZE)

4. Inside the Effects of Exercise: From Cellular to Psychological Benefits
   (https://youtu.be/an6LKlx3JH8)

5. 8 Minute Cardio Workout at Home
   (https://youtu.be/noDkFXX5r2Q)

6. Cardio vs. strength training: What you need to know
   (https://youtu.be/YvrKIQ_Tbsk)

7. Total Body Strength Training Without Weights for Women (https://youtu.be/mUns804YL5M)

# Chapter 8
# Your Diet

M uch of what we were taught about diet is flawed. People now appreciate that the food industry demonized fat and promoted sugar and wheat. We now understand that you don't get fat from eating fat any more than you get high cholesterol from eating cholesterol.

## The purpose of Eating

Every cell in your body needs a continuous supply of energy to power its cellular processes. This energy comes from the food we eat. Our body can survive on any kind of diet. The exception to this rule is a diet overloaded with protein. Protein overload is toxic because digestion of this amount of protein produces more ammonium than your kidneys can excrete. Symptoms of such a diet include diarrhea, fatigue, low blood pressure, headache, and a craving for fat. A diet of pure carbohydrates or fat doesn't produce biochemical problems like a pure protein diet.

## How Digestion Works

Digestion is the process that breaks down foods into the smallest components for the body to reassemble into complex molecules for internal use. This is important because food contains many toxic agents that we can't just let in safely. To understand the digestive process, we will start with the food in your mouth, and follow it through the entire gastrointestinal (GI) tract.

- ❑ **Mouth:** As you chew your food to break it down into smaller pieces, the saliva in your mouth contains enzymes that breakdown carbohydrates, proteins, and fats.
- ❑ **From Mouth to Stomach:** A series of contractions called peristalsis push food through the esophagus and into the stomach.
- ❑ **Stomach:** The stomach secretes hydrochloric acid that disinfects the food you eat.
- ❑ **Duodenum:** The duodenum connects the stomach to the small intestine. It continues to break down food using enzymes released by the pancreas and bile from the liver.
- ❑ **Liver:** The liver secretes a digestive juice called bile that helps digest fat and some vitamins. It also purifies the blood coming from the small intestine containing the absorbed nutrients before it travels to the rest of the body.
- ❑ **Pancreas:** The pancreas is the chief factory for digestive enzymes secreted into the duodenum. It also produces two opposing hormones, insulin and glucagon, to regulate your blood sugar level. When blood sugar is too high, the pancreas releases insulin to lower blood glucose by forcing it into cells to be used as energy or stored as fat. When blood sugar is too low, the pancreas produces glucagon, which raises the blood glucose by signaling the cells to make glucose from fat and glycogen.
- ❑ **Small Intestine:** The small intestine absorbs nutrients into the bloodstream. What's leftover (the waste) moves into the large intestine (large bowel or colon).
- ❑ **Large Intestine:** It takes about 36 hours for a stool to get through the colon. The stool itself is food debris

and bacteria. These bacteria perform several useful functions, such as synthesizing various vitamins, processing waste products, and protecting against harmful bacteria. When the descending colon becomes full of stool, it empties its contents into the rectum to begin the process of elimination.

# How Hunger Works

The **enteric nervous system** (ENS) is a network of 50 million nerve cells wrapping around the gut coordinating all complex digestive functions. It is in constant communication with the brain using hormones.

When your stomach is empty, its cells produce the hunger hormone **ghrelin** that tells the brain that you should eat something. When we eat a meal, the duodenum releases the hormone **cholecystokinin** to decrease appetite and stimulate the release of bile from the liver and digestive enzymes from the pancreas.

**Leptin** and **adiponectin** are hormones produced by your body's fat cells. Leptin tells your brain that—when you have enough fat stored—you don't need to eat and can burn calories at a normal rate. Adiponectin is involved in regulating glucose levels and fatty acid breakdown.

Lack of appetite control is not the root problem leading to obesity. Getting fatter results from stem cell aging, caused by telomere shortening and mutation across all cell types, particularly in cells of the liver, pancreas, and belly fat. Accumulation of genetic damage in these stem cells impairs our metabolic functions and leads to metabolic syndrome.

Eating the right diet can help you lengthen your telomeres and repair damaged DNA in these stem cells.

# Glycemic Index

Carbohydrates are the sugars, starches, and fibers found in fruits, grains, vegetables, and milk products. Your body breaks down the carbohydrates in your food into glucose and releases it into the bloodstream. Carbohydrates are classified as simple or complex, depending on the chemical structure and how quickly the sugar is absorbed into the bloodstream. The increase in blood sugar will stimulate the release of insulin that pushes the glucose into the cells to be used as energy or stored as fat. That's why sugary drinks and starchy food are a recipe for obesity.

The **glycemic index** (GI) ranks food by how much it raises blood glucose after it is eaten. Foods with a high GI increase blood glucose higher and faster than foods with a low GI.

To avoid storing fat, it is better to avoid high glycemic foods like sugary and starchy foods and eat lower glycemic foods like nuts, fruits, and vegetables.

Starting a century ago, the US government has published food pyramids to empower Americans to make healthy food choices. But the science behind these food pyramids is flawed, and the recommendations are rather arbitrary. For example, the 2011 pyramid suggests we take most of our diet from grains filled with high glycemic carbohydrates. Food pyramids are marketing hype, influenced by professional lobbyists because they had a lot of wheat, corn, and milk to sell to consumers. Ignore them.

# Telomere Science and Nutrition

### Studies agree: the Mediterranean diet is best

- ❏ Researchers from the Harvard School of Public Health say that eating Mediterranean-style diets appears to increase telomere length.
- ❏ A 5-year prospective study verifies the hypothesis of an anti-inflammatory Mediterranean diet that those who ate the lower inflammatory foods had the slowest rate of telomere shortening.

❑ Researchers in a cross-sectional study of elderly patients found that the intake of a Mediterranean diet was associated with telomerase activity levels.

❑ In a Chinese study of 556 patients with prediabetes, researchers found an association between poor glycemic control and shorter telomeres. The study also found that longer telomeres are associated with eating legumes, nuts, fish, and seaweeds. Total calories, higher fat and carb diets, cereals, and meats were associated with increased inflammation.

### *Processed meat causes inflammation and telomere shortening*

In a study published in *The American Journal of Clinical Nutrition*, researchers found that processed meats such as hot dogs, bacon, and lunch meats are harmful to your cells. The researchers found telomere shortening even in people who only ate processed meat once a week, compared with those who avoided it altogether.

### *Obesity is associated with shorter telomeres*

Researchers from the UK found that lean women had longer telomeres, while heavier women had much shorter ones. They also noted a direct relationship between leptin, a hormone associated with appetite and obesity, and shorter telomeres.

### *Do changing habits help our telomeres?*

As discussed in chapter 7, just deciding to improve eating habits triggers improvement even in the placebo group.

## TMT Eating Guidelines

❑ **Know the Mediterranean diet components**. Avoid excess sugar or carbs, which are glycemic and therefore fattening. Keep away from processed or factory-farmed animal products. Eat what agrees with your body and energizes you.

❏ **Manage your appetite**—keep healthy snacks available to eat like fruit and drink lots of water to suppress ghrelin.

❏ **Favor a plant-based diet**—like salads.

❏ **Practice intermittent fasting**. Daily fasting triggers cell death and intracellular waste clearance. If you skip breakfast and don't eat past 6 p.m., you can get a good 18 hours of cell turnover every day.

# Online Videos

1. Digestive System, Part 1
   (https://youtu.be/yIoTRGfcMqM)

2. Digestive System, Part 2
   (https://youtu.be/pqgcEIaXGME)

3. Digestive System, Part 3
   (https://youtu.be/jGme7BRkpuQ)

4. Hungry? Hunger Control, Cravings, Weight Loss, Nutrition (https://youtu.be/74_jgfVk7Xs)

5. One Easy Tip for Weight Loss, Belly Fat, Sugar Cravings, Blood Sugar, Diabetes, Glycemic Index?
   (https://youtu.be/vPi7zeTl8ww)

6. Mediterranean diet, our legacy, our future
   (https://youtu.be/1Aoj4awQb9g)

# Chapter 9
## Your Supplements

Your diet may not be optimal in providing your body with all the nutrients it needs. A dietary supplement is a product intended to supplement the diet. It can be vitamins, minerals, fibers, amino acids, fatty acids, and herbal extracts.

Sometimes, telomere/stem cell damage produces a nutrient deficiency that supplementation can't fix because the deficiency is the *result* and not the *cause* of the problem. In these cases, we must repair the damage that causes the deficiency.

### *Vitamins*

Vitamins are molecules that your body needs for certain chemical reactions. Deficiencies in these molecules will cause specific diseases. There are 13 recognized vitamins, but your body can only make vitamins D and K. So you must get the other 11 vitamins from your diet. We can do without vitamin supplementation as long as you eat a well-balanced diet rich in fruits and vegetables.

Excess vitamin supplementation is dangerous. The fat-soluble vitamins (A, D, E, and K) are stored in the body's fat tissues and can build up to toxic levels when consumed in excess. The other vitamins are water-soluble and will not build up in your body.

## Essential Minerals

A balanced diet contains many compounds with calcium, sodium, chloride, phosphorous, potassium, magnesium, selenium, copper, iron, and zinc that the body needs. Only people with chronic blood loss from gastrointestinal bleeding or excessive menstruation should need to supplement iron.

An exception is the element iodine, which the thyroid gland needs. Before the iodization of table salt in the 1920s, iodine intake was low in many areas without marine food sources. This led to thyroid deficiency and enlarged thyroid glands in the neck.

## Essential Fatty Acids

The body needs omega-3s and omega-6s to regulate inflammation and to make cell membranes, myelin (the fatty insulation covering our nerve cell's axons), and neurotransmitters. Mammals cannot make omega-3 or omega-6 fatty acids, but they are present in a wide range of foods such as fish, seeds, nuts, and eggs.

## Essential Amino Acids

Amino acids are the building blocks of proteins. The body needs 20 amino acids but can only synthesize 11. Essential amino acids are the 9 amino acids that our body can't synthesize. Some animal-based foods, such as fish, milk, eggs, chicken, pork, and beef contain all essential amino acids. Many plant-based foods, such as legumes, grains, soybeans, and some nuts and seeds also contain good amounts of protein. Vegetable sources of proteins are healthier than animal protein sources.

# Fad Supplements and How They Fail

## *Antioxidants*

Free radicals are unstable molecules that can damage cells, causing illness and aging. They are produced from normal essential metabolic processes in the human body or from exposure to cigarette smoking, radiation, and industrial chemicals. Antioxidants are substances that may protect your cells against the effects of free radicals. However, recent research has shown that lab animals that produce many free radicals live longer and that antioxidants, which reduce free radicals, do not prolong life.

## *CoQ10 and NADH*

Your body synthesizes coenzyme Q10 (CoQ10) and nicotinamide adenine dinucleotide hydride (NADH) to support mitochondrial functions. The declining levels of CoQ10 and NADH result from gene mutations, not aging, so supplementation can't fix them.

## *Resveratrol*

Resveratrol is an ingredient in red wine thought to improve insulin sensitivity, reduce risk of heart disease and increase longevity. Recent research shows that resveratrol does not offer these benefits in healthy women.

## *Probiotics*

Probiotics are friendly bacteria that you ingest to restore or rebalance your gut microbiome. But aberrations in the gut's microbial balance are rare. They are often caused by antibiotics or cleansers that induce extinction events, which allows for opportunistic newcomers to take hold, causing skin infections like MRSA (methicillin-resistant Staph aureus), infectious diarrhea, and vaginal infections.

One problem with probiotics is that the friendly bacteria that you purchase at the health food store can't survive stomach acids and digestive enzymes without protective encapsulation. Another problem is the rapid and efficient transit through sterile small intestines means there is nowhere to host them. The lactobacilli at the health food store are unstable and insignificant in numbers as bacterial occupants of the colon.

## Fecal Transplant

A fecal transplant involves transplanting feces from a healthy donor into another person to restore their gut microbial balance. Reintroducing good bacteria using a fecal transplant may help with C. difficile colitis caused by antibiotic use.

Bacterial vaginosis is a common condition in women caused by bacterial growth in the vagina, resulting in burning feelings, discharge, and a bad odor. Vaginal microbiota transplantation can often rebalance the vaginal microbial ecosystem.

## Hormone Supplementation

Many athletes use **anabolic steroids** to increase muscle mass, but they come with many risks, such as acne, baldness, aggression, masculinization, testicular atrophy, and menstrual irregularity.

**Human growth hormone** (HGH) is a popular supplement for anti-aging aficionados and bodybuilders. They also come with many risks, such as fluid retention, joint and muscle pain, carpal tunnel syndrome, high blood sugar, and cancer.

Our sex hormones of **estrogen** and **testosterone** decline as we age. Studies have shown hormone replacement—estrogen for women and testosterone for men—benefits older people. The benefits include better sleep, enhanced sexual and exercise performance, higher rates of energy, improved mood, and increased health markers.

### *Herbs Are Bioactive Cocktails*

Factors to consider when supplementing with herbs:

- ❏ Safety and purity are critical. Seek certificates of authenticity that show organic farming and lack of pesticides and harmful contaminants like lead, mercury, and infectious agent.
- ❏ Learn all you can about the benefits of the supplement you are taking.
- ❏ Experiment with how you feel because a placebo or biochemical effect might vary from person to person.

### *Herbal Telomerase Activators*

TA-65 is a plant-based compound that can help maintain or rebuild telomeres. Studies show that TA-65 doesn't increase the telomerase enzyme, but it takes you into a state of better flow, balance, and healing.

### *Adaptogenic Herbs*

Adaptogens are non-toxic plants that are marketed as helping the body resist stressors of all kinds, whether physical, chemical or biological. But they produce different effects on different people depending on their physiology—they might make one person sleepy and another alert.

# What Are Common Nutritional Supplement Deficiencies?

As long as you iodize your salt and have access to fruits, nuts, vegetables, and fish, you should not have supplemental nutrient deficiencies. But there are conditions where you need supplementation.

❑ If you have dark skin and live in northern latitudes, you may need to supplement with vitamin D owing to poor ultraviolet light absorption.

❑ Vegetarians should supplement with vitamin B12 because their dietary intake is often too low, causing anemia or low blood count.

❑ People who consume the same processed foods daily (for example, instant ramen) are at risk for nutritional supplement deficiencies.

❑ Pregnant women should protect their unborn fetuses with folic acid, calcium, and omega-3 fatty acid.

❑ Excessive intake of calcium is dangerous. If the bone cells are not storing calcium because of telomere-induced damage to those stem cells, no amount of calcium supplementation will change that.

❑ If you feel tired or cold, have a slow heart rate, dry skin, and constipation, you might have a low thyroid hormone level. Iodine supplementation can improve your situation. If your thyroid cells are senescent and damaged and your pituitary/hypothalamic regulation is faulty, intermittent fasting and curcumin can help clear the damaged cells to restore balance.

❑ You can't raise your magnesium levels with oral supplementation. The only change between taking magnesium and placebo was the amount of magnesium in the urine, not the blood. The problem lies in damaged stem cells that affect the magnesium levels in the blood.

## What Supplements Are Best to Take?

If you have limited meat consumption, supplement with vitamin B12.

Calcium supplementation is healthy in small doses.

If you don't add iodized salt, you need to get it from seafood, yogurt, or turkey breast.

We recommend sex hormone replacement for older folks.

Telomerase activators supplements and other adaptogenic herbs may help you to stay healthy, happy, and live longer.

## Online Videos

1. Supplements that lengthen telomeres
   (https://youtu.be/FaCaZQ7q3p4)

2. Hormone Therapy & Anti-Aging
   (https://youtu.be/U8_Xjg0W6oo)

3. Hormone Replacement Therapy
   (https://youtu.be/YblHq9dD22s)

# Part 3

## The TeloMirror Plan in Action

# Chapter 10
# Your TeloMirror Tune-Up

N ow that you have mastered all six TeloMirror Tools of breathing, mindset, sleep, exercise, diet, and supplements, let's put them to use in your individualized plan.

## Daily Self-Inventory

Use the worksheet in the appendix to take a daily inventory of how you breathe, think, sleep, exercise, and eat.

## Compiling the Data

Once you have accumulated eight straight days of TMT self-inventory, you will compile your data and look for patterns.

### Sleep Review

#### Last Thoughts before Sleep

- ❏ **See if there was a correlation** between lack of sleep the night before and the following day's quality of life assessment.
- ❏ **If you recalled and recorded your dreams** in the morning, then try to correlate them with your last thoughts before going to sleep.

❏ **Cross out any negative pre-sleep thoughts** on your pages. Then for each negative thought, write out an antitoxin belief.

### Homework—Choose the seeds you'll sow

❏ Write a list of your favorite thoughts before sleep. Construct some antidote paradigms and positive affirmations to supplant your daily worries.

### Early to Bed?

❏ Time spent in bed, such as reading a book, does *NOT* count as sleep time. Your bedtime is the time you fell asleep.

### Time of Waking?

❏ What time did you wake up? Staying up all night on work and school commitments hurts your productivity and circadian rhythm afterward. If you have to wake up early, then go to bed earlier or take a nap the following day.

### Total Hours/Cycles?

❏ 4 cycles (6 hours) of sleep is the bare minimum.
❏ If you are operating at 3 cycles (4S hours), you may suffer from a sleep-induced Dunning-Kruger effect that you don't even know you are impaired.
❏ If you are getting 5 cycles (7S hours), you are ok. I recommend you go to sleep an hour earlier. It may help your telomeres and prevent Alzheimer's, obesity, and other diseases.
❏ If you are getting 6 cycles (8S hours), congratulations! You are doing the least that your body needs to repair those telomeres.
❏ If you are getting 7 or more cycles (9S + hours), you will enjoy better telomeres. You may have fewer

wakeful hours, but you might enhance their quality re-
garding joy and productivity.

### Homework—Make the time for sleep

❑ Go through your records to find out why you got to
sleep too late or woke up too early. As you balance
your daily rituals, try to always make room for a nine-
hour block of time.

### Notes: Troubles with sleep

❑ If you have trouble getting to sleep, go back to chapter 6 to review how to optimize your environment. If
you have vivid dreams, note their content. There will
be answers to unresolved issues and your dreams often have a high correlation with the last thoughts you
had before sleep, positive or negative.

## Breathing and Meditation Review

If you spend any time thinking about your breathing, that counts
as a mini-meditation. Whenever you feel anything untoward, you
can restore balance and presence by breathing deeply and mind-
fully. Find a technique to sit comfortably, fingertips touching,
eyes closed, and thoughts flowing freely as you consciously
breathe. Clear the clutter of ego identification, audit those automatic thoughts, reframe them with gratitude and enjoy the
present moment.

## Exercise Review

Reflect upon what physical activity made you most joyful and
that will guide you to increase the time for those activities.

## *Eating Review*

As you examine the meals you have, what patterns emerge? Can you imagine changes that will increase enjoyment, quality, variety, and meaning?

## **Supplements Review**

Did you take your daily required supplements? If you take lots of multiple supplements, consider stopping them all and then adding them back, one at a time, to see what the effects are.

## *Review the Speed Bump of Life*

### Conflict, self-loathing, projecting anger, and anxiety

- ❏ What events or thoughts produced conflict, self-loathing, anger, and anxiety? For each, ask yourself three questions:
- ❏ Was it **REAL** (or mostly in my head)?
- ❏ Was it an **ANT** (automatic negative thought)?
- ❏ What is the **JUDO MOVE** (reframing with gratitude) that I can summon the next time this happens?

### Bonding, blessings, achievements, gratitude, optimism

- ❏ Note the improvements in relationships you had, the unexpected delights, the goals achieved, the gratitude you felt, and the moments of unbridled hope. The more you focus on these things over discernment and scarcity, the more light you invite into your life.

### Enjoyment

- ❏ Did you enjoy yourself on this wonderful day? Even in the darkest and most powerless moments, take comfort in knowing that you always have the choice of how you react and where and how we will encounter joy.

### Authenticity

❑ If you resist the temptation to agree with people just to get along, give yourself an A!

### Presence

❑ Were you focused and aware throughout the day or did your thoughts stray toward regrets of the past or worries about the future?

### Productivity

❑ Did you make progress that will get you closer to your goals?

### Gratitude

❑ Did you express it to someone? If you did, did it transform your relationship to a higher level?

### Self-Compassion

❑ Self-compassion is extending compassion to yourself in instances of perceived inadequacy, failure, or general suffering. If you need to feel self-compassion in the midst of despair, try to get outside yourself like Ebenezer Scrooge from *A Christmas Carol.* Imagine you died yesterday. Now use your imagination and visit the people in your life. Are they happy that you are gone?

## Your Strengths and Challenges

If you were able to complete the inventory for last week, you now know how your six TMTs are functioning. Spend some time with your eight days of data and refer back to earlier chapters and their recommendations and optimize your TMT.

## Continuous Improvement

Instead of weekly, refer back every night to the day's inventory, and do your homework. In time, your ability to run the self-inventory will become so automatic that you will do it without pen and paper. You can remember these 16 inventory items:

- ❏ Thoughts before sleep
- ❏ Time to bed
- ❏ Time of waking
- ❏ Hours slept
- ❏ Meditation
- ❏ Exercise
- ❏ Meals
- ❏ Negative things
- ❏ Positive things
- ❏ Supplements
- ❏ Enjoyment
- ❏ Authenticity
- ❏ Presence
- ❏ Productivity
- ❏ Gratitude
- ❏ Self-compassion

I recommend taking a few minutes to do the self-inventory every night.

## Online Videos

1. The Dunning-Kruger Effect - Cognitive Bias - Why Incompetent People Think They Are Competent (https://youtu.be/y50i1bI2uN4)

2. Signs of Sleep Deprivation (https://youtu.be/vzgYD_EZIvY)

# Appendix

**TeloMirror Self-Inventory**

(Day _____)

Sleep (best recorded when you first wake up):

Last thoughts before my last night's sleep:

_____

Time I went to sleep: _____

Time I awoke: _____

Total hours slept and # of 90-minute cycle_____

~4S hours or less equals 3 cycles or less

~6 hours equals 4 cycles

~7S hours equals 5 cycles

~8S hours equals 6 cycles

~9S+ hours equals 7+ cycles

Sleep Notes (e.g., trouble getting to sleep, awakenings and what woke you, and any vivid dreams):

_____

Conscious breathing or meditation done today: _____

Exercise done (times and type):_____

Eating (with whom and what I ate):

Breakfast:_____

Snack:_____

Lunch: _____

Snack:_____

Dinner: _____

Snack:_____

Supplements taken: _____

Notes on any memorable conflicts, self-loathing, anger, or anxiousness:

_____

Notes on any memorable bonding, blessings, achievements, gratitude, optimism:

_____

Quality of life assessment:
Give yourself a  grade of A  to F  for this day with respect to
EnJoyment _____
Authenticity _____
Presence_____
Productivity _____
Gratitude_____
Self-compassion _____

Source: Ed Park, MD, *The Telomere Miracle* (2018)

# Index

# About the Author

Lee Tang is a retired executive of a major global insurance company. Prior to his retirement, he has worked as an actuary, a risk officer, and a chief financial officer for several major insurance organizations in the United States, Canada, and Taiwan.

## *Plea from the Author*

Hey, Reader. So you got to the end of my book. I hope that means you enjoyed it. Whether or not you did, I would just like to thank you for giving me your valuable time to entertain you. I am blessed to have such a fulfilling job, but I have that job only because of people like you; people kind enough to give my books a chance and spend their hard-earned money buying them. For that, I am eternally grateful.

If you would like to discover more about my other books then please visit my website for full details. You can find it at https://lmtpress.wordpress.com

Also feel free to contact me by email (leetang888@gmail.com), as I would love to hear from you.

If you enjoyed this book and would like to help, then you could think about leaving a review—even if it's only a line or two—on your favorite bookstore, Goodreads, or other sites; and talk about the book with your friends. The most important part of how well a book sells is how many positive reviews it has, so if you leave me one then you are directly helping me to continue this journey as a full-time writer. Thanks in advance to anyone who does. It means a lot.

Lee Tang

# Also by Lee Tang

## Standalones

**Dual Momentum Trend Trading:** *How to Avoid Costly Trading Mistakes and Make More Money in the Stock, ETF, Futures and Forex Markets with This Simple and Reliable Swing Trading Strategy.*

**Canada's Public Pension System Made Simple:** *The Secrets To Maximizing Your Retirement Income From Government Pensions*

## Summary & Study Guide Series

1. **Summary & Study Guide - Brain Maker:** *The Power of Gut Microbes to Heal and Protect Your Brain-Including Diet Cheat Sheet*

2. **Summary & Study Guide - The Gene:** *An Intimate History*

3. **Summary & Study Guide - The Emperor of All Maladies:** *A Biography of Cancer*

4. **Summary & Study Guide - NeuroTribes:** *The Legacy of Autism*

5. **Summary & Study Guide - Brain Storms:** *The Race to Unlock the Secrets of Parkinson's Disease*

6. **Summary & Study Guide - The End of Diabetes:** *The Eat to Live Plan to Prevent and Reverse Diabetes-Including Diet Cheat Sheet*

7. **Summary & Study Guide - The End of Heart Disease:** *The Eat to Live Plan to Prevent and Reverse Heart Disease-Including Diet Cheat Sheet*

8. **Summary & Study Guide - ADHD Nation:** *Anatomy of An Epidemic - Attention-Deficit/Hyperactivity Disorder*

9. **Summary & Study Guide - The Obesity Code:** *Unlocking the Secrets of Weight Loss*

For a complete list of books by Lee Tang and information about the author, visit *https://lmtpress.wordpress.com.*

Made in the USA
Middletown, DE
11 September 2022

10196361R00046